Disgust: A Memoir

Stephanie Grant

For my loves,
A & J & A

And in memory of Richard McCann

Disgust: A Memoir

The body, as we have tried to show, provides a basic scheme for all symbolism.

MARY DOUGLAS[1]

1 The Man Who Would Not Kiss

1.1

When, in my twenties, I came out to my parents as a lesbian, I became an object of their disgust. I was not surprised by their recoiling, as they were devout Catholics, but I was still distraught. As a result, I worked to eliminate disgust from my repertoire of emotions. Yet, as of late, I've noticed the feeling is on the rise in me: I experience it more and more as I age. And, it must be said, disgust overwhelmed the public square in the months and years following the 2016 presidential election.

1.2

Researchers have identified three types, or domains, of disgust: pathogenic, sexual, and moral.[1] Common to all three is the fear of contagion. Of course, the different types can overlap: the germophobe who refuses any kissing—philemaphobia—might also register a strong sense of either moral or sexual disgust; that is, she or he might experience one form of disgust intensifying the other.

1.3

Years ago, I dated, or—let me be frank—tried to bed a man who suffered from philemaphobia. It is difficult, in retrospect, to describe how desirous I was of this man, given that his avoidance of kissing would have proven a serious impediment to my own sexual arousal. But isn't it always nearly impossible, in retrospect, to explain desire? Besides, he played hard to get, extremely so, which served as its own very effective form of arousal.

1.4

Now I wonder whether his pathogenic disgust was born of sexual disgust, as it served as a kind of roadblock in his pursuit of women. I say a *kind of* roadblock because he was reasonably sexually successful, having been married three times and having fathered four children; in other words, his fear of kissing was not an insurmountable impediment for him or for the women he married. It's also possible that his pathogenic disgust functioned as a kind of moral disgust: he was married when I met him and seemed ambivalent about stepping out on his third wife, as his infidelities had ended his two previous marriages.

1.5

I, myself, did not feel disgust—moral, sexual or pathogenic—at the thought of sleeping with a married man. I know a lot of people do.

1.6

A few years prior, my partner and I had opened our relationship because we had stopped having sex altogether. Alas, this is not an unusual circumstance in long-term relationships; among lesbians, it has a name: lesbian bed death. Although we are hardly the only couples thus afflicted, we are—as far as I know—the only community to have named the affliction. My partner and I lived without sex for five years before taking the step of pursuing others while maintaining the emotional primacy of our partnership as well as our commitment, as parents, to each other and to our daughters.

The man with philemaphobia was a practicing Catholic who spent most of his adult life in the military. He was the first contemporary of mine with whom I'd enjoyed meaningful conversation who'd been in a theater of war. He'd been in several, including Iraq I, Afghanistan, Iraq II. I was stunned, and frankly impressed, by this fact, though not in a gushing, fan-girl way. While an active soldier, he belonged to a famous Army infantry division that parachuted into war zones. He'd shot at people and been shot at. I found it nearly impossible to integrate these last facts into my experience of him, which I believe is the definition of cognitive dissonance.

1.8

Once, in an email conversation, he explained to me how to run to evade being shot and killed, which involves moving to a count of three: *I am up, he sees me, I am down. I am up, he sees me, I am down.* I was grateful to learn this for two reasons: first, because it had been an essential part of his life—this dodging of bullets—and his willingness to discuss it made our tenuous connection more intimate; and second, because I sensed that in some unnameable American future I might need this strategy.

1.9

The human body offers us significant opportunities for disgust—its eruptions and excreta, its certain, inescapable decay.[2] Part of what makes disgust such a powerful, visceral experience is the fear that the disgusting thing will, or has already, corrupted us.[3] Part of what makes disgust central to our moral machinery is our sense that stabilizing norms have been violated: some object or person is in the wrong place—the proverbial hair in the soup.[4] According to this logic, disgust erupts when the categories and oppositions that structure our daily experience fail to stay distinct: clean vs. filthy; inside vs. outside; male vs. female; us vs. them.

1.10

In the weeks that followed my coming out to my parents, they expressed their disgust in different ways. My mother applied what she believed about the category *lesbian*—lonely, perverse, a danger to children—to the category *Stephanie*, whereas I had been hoping she would do the reverse, allowing her experience of me to revise her understanding of lesbians. My father, who was verbally more reticent than my mother, yet who was in possession of an emotionally expressive colon, suffered a bout of diarrhea. This is difficult to acknowledge, let alone commit to paper, as the appearance of feces might provoke the reader's own disgust, and she might then turn away from this particular manifestation of turning away. Researchers have dubbed feces "the universal disgust object"[5] because its intimate foulness reminds us of our inevitable decay, our unbearable animal vulnerability.

1.11

Both my parents' responses were very painful—
excruciating, in fact—and, as I've said, from thereon
in, I tried to eliminate disgust from my feeling life.
At the time, I believed this gesture to have political,
which is to say, moral meaning; and, to a certain extent,
it did: feeling disgust establishes one's superiority
over the object or person one is disgusted by.[6]

1.12

Until 2017, we'd never had a president who so frequently articulated his feelings of disgust for so many. Because it ranks those involved, thereby creating hierarchies among people, the feeling of disgust challenges the democratic ideal of universal equality, which, although imperfectly realized in our country is much acclaimed by its citizens.

1.13

My partner and I did not stop having sex because we were disgusted by one another; we stopped having sex because we were enraged with one another. She was enraged because she experienced me as a greedy and callous lover who did not attend to her needs. I was enraged because I felt I could never, no matter the attention I paid, please her. As judgmental and unkind as these assessments sound, they were both, to a certain extent, accurate. They were also a form of collusion.

Collusion is not uncommon in long-term relationships; it occurs when each person permanently occupies one side, one pole, of an argument. My therapist, whom I saw for something like 15 years when I lived in New York, and who was, of course, a Freudian, taught me about collusion. By refusing to contemplate any shift in their position, both partners prevent change; indeed, change becomes impossible. Which, it turns out, is the goal of collusion: stasis.

1.15

My partner and I ended our collusion around sex when we began having sex with other people. Although we did not abandon our beliefs about how and why our sexual life had become broken, we each felt, in pursuing others, returned to our sexual selves. Almost immediately, we stopped being enraged with one another. To our mutual surprise, once we accepted fully the devastating loss of our sexual relationship, our furious resentments lifted, and we were flooded with gratitude.

1.16

Gratitude is, if not a form of love, one of our best means of practicing it.

My sister christened the man who would not kiss
The Spy, because of his high security clearance: he
had retired from the military and was working in the
defense industry when we met. She, god bless her,
spent several years in a relationship with someone
who suffered from philemaphobia and suggested I
stay away. This was an excellent suggestion, but it
turns out that I am not good at: 1) taking suggestions;
2) postponing desire; 3) taking suggestions about
postponing desire.

1.18

That sounds like an Oliver Sacks title, doesn't it? *The Man Who Would Not Kiss.*

I think it's possible that women, in general, disgusted The Spy, although I don't know this for a fact. He was fully aware of the irony present in his fear of kissing given his many years of demonstrating physical bravery in theaters of war. Indeed, many Army shrinks had pointed out what they saw as a causal link between the two: in order not to be afraid when at war, he had redirected his fear onto something infinitely more controllable: his wife. Or wives. His women.

1.20

A friend in whom I confided my attraction said we were hothouse flowers to each other, compelling because so utterly strange. Although he knew many lesbians, being for so many years in the military, he did not know many lesbian writers who were feminist, who had children, who had sex with men, and who lived mostly in queer worlds.

I, on the other hand, knew nothing about the conservative military worlds in which he circulated. For instance: almost all the women with whom he had sex wanted to marry him. They wanted him to take care of them materially, to provide them with children, houses, swimming pools and other proofs of status and wealth. During one of our rare dinners, he spent a lot of time telling me about the property he had purchased, the advantageous financial deals he had made. I could not have been more bored until it occurred to me that he was flirting. I had no idea how to flirt *in response* to this information: advertise my own (significant) financial inadequacies? Was that what heterosexual women did? For his part, The Spy was perplexed that I professed interest only in sex. Indeed, he found my behavior deeply suspicious. I'm pretty sure he thought that I, too, was a spy.

1.22

Imagine! Me, a spy!

Once, in an intimate conversation that I hoped would be a prelude to sex, he referred to my pubic hair as my *lady garden*. It was an expression I had never heard before, and I almost burst out laughing when he used it. Fortunately, I was alone—we were communicating by text—as I wouldn't want to laugh at a lover's sex talk, no matter how alien. It occurred to me then that conventional sexual language—words like *pussy* and *cunt*—might have disgusted him because he used those words with his Army buddies; that is, he used those words to disparage men who didn't perform well as soldiers (I had heard him do so) and therefore did not like to use those words with the women whom he fucked but would not kiss.

1.24

The word *pussy* to mean *vagina* has become part of public discourse because the ex-President was caught on tape bragging that he frequently grabbed women "by the pussy." I don't believe the category *president* has as its antithesis *sexual predator*, but surely some of my disgust at 45 reflects his having violated a category that had otherwise seemed relatively stable to me.

Lately, I have found myself wondering whether the former President, a self-described germophobe, might suffer from philemaphobia. This seems unlikely given his boasts about kissing, or trying to kiss, women with whom he was not already intimate. Perhaps it is intimacy itself that provokes his dread. Theorists are not in agreement about what feeling is the precise opposite of disgust. Some say love, others trust.

If disgust is fundamentally a fear of corruption, it seems possible that The Spy was afraid to kiss women because of the fear of becoming one, which is to say, the fear of becoming a soldier who did not perform well, that is, a *pussy*. Which would have endangered his life. It could be that he experienced kissing—rather than fucking—as destabilizing to the categories male and female. This is an interesting idea to contemplate: why kissing? Wouldn't intercourse, with its well-known intensity, be a more likely candidate? Perhaps kissing destabilizes because, when we kiss, we are, necessarily, face to face and must see one another? Perhaps kissing because, when we see one another in a sexual embrace, we witness the collapse—or near collapse—of otherwise stable, and dear, categories: inside vs. outside, animal vs. human, you vs. me.

Or perhaps kissing destabilizes because, when we kiss someone new to us—I mean, really kiss someone, for the first time—aren't we all behaving, just a little bit, like spies?

I wonder if I, myself, did not feel disgust at the idea of sleeping with a married man because I do not identify with the category *heterosexual*. Which immediately begs the question: why was a thoughtful lesbian like myself pursuing sex with a man? I'm not sure I can answer this, although I have some theories. So do many people in my life. Have theories.

According to Freud, disgust is essential to desire. The disgust we feel about sexual activity is a repression of our desire, and the repression functions like a dam; once enough repressed feeling is built up, it overwhelms the dam.[7] Another way of thinking about this is that sexual intimacy is forged when we put aside our sexual disgust.[8] I can remember, quite vividly, moments of overcoming my own sexual disgust: of penises, for example, which are naturally disgusting to both women and men. Or so Freud said.

At some point, I was so desirous of sleeping with The Spy, who was so clearly suspicious of me, and so deftly keeping me at arm's length, I considered asking him to buy me some expensive jewelry. Perhaps if he saw that my wanting to sleep with him contained, and thereby disguised, my desire to be taken care of financially, he would be less suspicious. He seemed to believe that no woman would be willing to overcome her "natural" (to him and to Freud) disgust of sexual activity if not, in some material way, compensated.

In my twenties, I had a girlfriend who was a sensational kisser. Sometimes, she would hold my face in her hands, so that I could not turn away, and kiss me with great force. *I'm fucking your mouth*, she would say. Perhaps because of this, nowadays, during sex, I can sometimes (*some*times) have an orgasm simply from being kissed. Which brings me back, rather emphatically, to the question, already posed, but not yet answered: why on earth would I want to have sex with a man who would not kiss?

Obviously, I hate this question; I hate it because the answer seems, well, obvious—and frankly humiliating: I wanted to be desired by him. I wanted his desire to become so strong that, like the water bursting the dam, it overcame his many reservations: the threat to his marriage; the damage to his self-esteem that another failed marriage would engender; my potential spy-ness; his terrible fear of kissing. Alas, I wanted the confirmation of my attractiveness that his desire would convey. And I wanted to leave behind, if only temporarily, the punishing category, so well-known to me, of ugly dyke.

1.33

It will likely come as no surprise that The Spy and I are no longer in touch. Our shared experiment at intimacy with an ideological opposite ended, as virtual couplings so often do, via a slow attrition of interest. For a while, we continued to exchange the occasional text, but, after the 2016 presidential election, I grew wary of discovering for whom he had voted. Not knowing has allowed me to remain grateful for everything that our brief courtship taught me about myself and about the world.

Indeed, my flirtation with The Spy allowed me to observe myself in moments of cognitive dissonance —perhaps, themselves, moments of disgust—when my internal beliefs were contradicted by new information, and to see how I overcame them, whether by re-thinking where I started (as I had wished, all those years ago, my mother had done) or by removing myself from what I found so very disturbing. The former is more difficult than the latter, but worthwhile, even necessary, if we are to know ourselves truly. In this way, disgust will reveal to us, for better or worse, for better *and* worse, our deepest held values.

As time passes, and disgust becomes more central to the political life of our nation, my gratitude toward The Spy only intensifies. The unnameable American future that I've long feared seems irrevocably at hand, and I find myself wondering, not whether, but in what context I will need to make use of the strategy The Spy so unselfconsciously offered me. I wonder when I, or someone I hold dear, will need to respond evasively—perhaps fleeing some form of militarized police or, equally possible, some form of militarized hate-group; when will I, when will we need to run for our lives, saying as we run: *I am up, he sees me, I am down. I am up, he sees me, I am down.*

2 Some Things that Disgust Me

2.1

Genus *rattus*—order *rodentia*—which is to say, rats generally. Specifically, a rat in my house, not small, more medium-sized, skulking along the baseboard, brazen, plain as day, that hunched comportment, as if tensing its shoulders, readying itself, the long, pink, pointed nose, and too-long tail. One night, impossibly, a possum, under the dining room table, back lit, the same menacing silhouette and long, pink, animate tail. *How did that freaking thing*—all its fur-less parts (nose, ears, the little, busy paws) more intensely pink, what you might call, if you were Joyce Carol Oates, sexual organ pink, writing about women and men, writing about purity and danger. *How did that freaking thing enter our house, our lives?*

Disgust is matter out of place, says anthropologist Mary Douglas, in the wrong place, dirt not necessarily dirty when outside. Also, the reverse: inside things suddenly out, suddenly on display, like entrails say, or tissue and bone. That time the college basketball player's leg broke on national TV, the bone piercing the skin, his teammates, coaches, cameras all turned away shaking, shook, doubled over in disgust at the body envelope of Kevin Ware broken open, exposed to the dirty, dirty air. Possums are marsupials but, like rodents, make their bodies follow wherever they push their heads.

2.3

If our bodies are envelopes housing us, our persons, the skin is the body envelope's envelope. My daughter with a tiny screwdriver takes apart brightly colored plastic pencil sharpeners to liberate the tiny razors trapped inside. She shaves her skin in parallel lines, peeling away her self-disgust one layer at a time. At night, unable to sleep, I wonder what possum-out-of-place, what inside out, what outside in, what genus *rattus*, has provoked her disgust? Unable to sleep, unable to read more Joyce Carol Oates, I sit hunched at the dining room table, tensing my shoulders, readying myself, my long, pink, animate tail, my little, busy paws, waiting for her disgust to metamorphose, like mine, into rage.

3 Self-Disgust

3.1

It's true that my mother was disgusted by my lesbianism, but years before, when I was just a child, she was disgusted by all of us, her three children and her husband. When she was very angry—in a rage—she called us *disgusting* or *disgusting pigs*. Because she suffered from depression, she was angry much of the time, although this language usually announced the outer edge of her fury: a shaming of last resort.

3.2

The Freudian therapist once told me that depression was anger turned inward, but I don't know if this idea is still *au courant*, so far have we moved away from psychoanalytic models in favor of medical ones. In my mother's case, she was adept at turning her anger outward, at the four of us, a gesture for which, according to my therapist's logic, I should be grateful; but find, alas, that I am not.

3.3

My mother's depression arrived soon after my brother, her first child, was born. She cried all day, refused to dress, could not take care of the baby. The grandmothers were brought in—this was 1955—and she was sent to St. Elizabeth's Hospital in Brighton, Massachusetts, for electroconvulsive therapy. None of us children knew about her illness until after she died.

3.4

Initially my mother's treatment was outpatient: she was shocked, then sent home to her many responsibilities. One day, according to my dad, she refused to get in the car to go for treatment, and so was hospitalized. Committed? I don't know if they used that word.

3.5

I have not found it especially difficult to integrate this new information about my mother into my understanding of her. Although surprised when I learned of her illness, I did not experience cognitive dissonance. Mostly, I experienced relief that the mystery of who she was had been solved.

3.6

Lately, I try to imagine myself into her experience: 28 years old, devoutly Catholic, less than two years married, newly a mother and newly a failure at being one. I try to imagine what she said to herself, how she narrated her decision to try ECT, which was administered, at the time, without anesthesia and at high enough levels to break bones and smash teeth.

3.7

Interestingly, researchers have noted that depressed subjects more readily identify disgust in the facial expressions of others.[1] Some have conjectured a feedback loop between the two: the depressed person observes disgust in the faces of friends, family, and acquaintances, and concludes that *she* is the object of their disgust. This realization leads to self-disgust, and self-disgust takes the form of more (increased) depression.

3.8

Another way to say this might be that self-disgust *is* depression.

3.9

The disgust/depression feedback loop seems chicken-and-egg-ish to me: which came first? This might be the nature of all feedback loops: we are always looping, never beginning. Never quite at the start of something.

3.10

When she was 13, my daughter K was diagnosed with depression, and its contemporary analogue anxiety, after she tried to kill herself. During a harrowing, three-year period she was hospitalized multiple times. The first hospitalization took place after she tried to kill herself when she was 13. That evening has a quality of unreality to it, as if it happened to someone else's daughter, and I am privy only to the story's telling. After dinner, I stepped out to run an errand and, when I returned, K was pacing in front of our house. She told me that she needed to go to the ER because she had taken some of her other mom's ADHD medication. She was agitated and could hardly meet my gaze. When I asked how many pills, she said she didn't know. Five pills? I prompted. Ten? She shrugged. *Thirty maybe. Maybe forty.*

3.11

At the hospital, I was quickly, although not unkindly, separated from K. I did not object to the separation, nor to the scrutiny that I received, which was clearly intended to gauge my culpability in my daughter's attempt to destroy herself. I sat vigil in a chair just outside the room where K was examined. When the nurses changed her out of her street clothes and into the paper hospital scrubs she would wear for the next several days, they discovered that she had been cutting her arms and legs. A nurse cracked open the door and craned her neck in my direction: *Did you know about the cutting?* I did not.

3.12

As counterintuitive as it may sound, I think both K and I were relieved by the separation. She was relieved to have relinquished responsibility for her physical self—half a dozen nurses and doctors streamed in and out of the examination room, caring for her—and relieved, too, not to have to witness my response to what she'd done. I was relieved because the separation helped me accept the slight formality that had established itself between us during the drive to the hospital.

3.13

In the car, I remember thinking, with surprise: *I am not you.* For the first time in her 13 years, she had done something, experienced something that I had not already done, and she was headed somewhere I'd never been. I don't mean she seemed incomprehensible to me or that I could not accept her actions. Her suicide attempt was not estranging, and my feelings were not a protest. They were simply the sudden, visceral realization that we were not the same person. Which motherhood, at times, obscures.

3.14

"There are a number of life situations in which the weakening of disgusts regularly occurs. A mother's disgust is weaker for the body wastes of her infants. Between lovers, there is sometimes a loss of disgust for sexual secretions and body odors. In both cases, adaptation or extinction caused by frequent exposure may provide a satisfactory account. However, another interesting and more cognitive mechanism may be involved. The mother-child and lover relations involve, to some extent, a weakening or destruction of self boundaries. Because disgust critically involves things foreign to the self, these intimate relations may weaken disgust by blurring the self-other distinction." [2]

Before I was separated from K at the hospital, the triage nurse asked whether or not she was hearing voices. I was shocked by the casualness of the question—When was your last period? Are you experiencing pain anywhere in your body right now? Are you hearing voices? When K shook her head, No, I felt acute relief. Hearing voices is a form of hallucination—a tear in the fabric of the universe—frequently (although not universally) determined to be an instance of psychosis.

3.16

Cutting one's own skin is not considered psychotic behavior; rather, it is understood as a behavior that regulates mood. When the cutter is confronted with intolerable feelings—feelings that threaten to overwhelm or destroy her, or feelings that seem as though they might never abate—she cuts, or tears at, her skin, the body's envelope, in order to bring herself back to the state before the escalation of feelings began. That is, to bring herself back to herself.

3.17

In my mother's time, psychosis was described as *having a nervous breakdown*. There is something temporary, even literary-sounding, about this expression, as if psychosis were the equivalent of a good and possibly generative cry, after which one felt much better and was able to return to daily life, such as it was, writing poems, perhaps, or caring for children.

3.18

Take the baby, my mother told my father in 1955. *Take the baby and go find another wife.*

3.19

These juxtapositions of my daughter's illness and my mother's are not meant to draw a hereditary link between them; indeed K is not biologically related to me or to my mother, who died eight years before she was born. My partner gave birth to K and to her sister Q, who were conceived, as is not uncommon these days, using a sperm bank.

3.20

Also not uncommon these days: it took two years for my partner to conceive. As part of the endless insemination process, we read many (many) sperm donor profiles. These included inane questions that were meant, we supposed, to reveal personality: What is your favorite animal? Favorite color? Favorite food? Questions meant to suggest intelligence: What were your SAT scores? And those intended to disqualify: What is your religion? We spent most of our time scrutinizing the donors' health histories: I was vigilant about eliminating those whose profiles revealed evidence of mental illness.

3.21

What strikes me now about those absurd profiles—
one included a mini-diatribe from a young man who
protested the possibility that his sperm might be used
to help lesbians conceive; and which required I spend
several hours convincing my partner that, No, it
would not be delicious retribution to choose him for
this very reason—it took reading these profiles for
us to realize fully that both of our mothers had been
institutionalized for depression.

3.22

I say, *realize fully*, because the facts were not unknown to us. My partner has always been aware of her mother's depression, although the details—exactly what provoked her involuntary hospitalization—are fuzzy. She was in the process of leaving her husband and three children in order to pursue her career as an artist when she experienced moments of psychosis that involved speaking back to the television.

One part of my mother-in-law's story gets recounted with something like pleasure: in the famous New York psychiatric hospital to which she was sent, she met the writer JJ who was also having an art-related breakdown, and they became life-long friends. Neither my mother-in-law, nor her new writer friend, underwent ECT—at least, not to my knowledge. Although their hospitalizations took place fewer than ten years after my mother's, these women were afforded different treatment options. College-educated and part of New York's bohemian art scene, my mother-in-law and JJ were also likely to have read Betty Freidan's *The Feminine Mystique*, which came out in 1963, four years before they were hospitalized, and which gave voice to the "problem that has no name." Indeed, they became participants in, and beneficiaries of, the revolution that followed. Which is to say, both women had the means to understand their illness as something other than personal failure. Whereas my working-class, Catholic mother did not.

3.24

"[I]n the 1950s ECT became a staple treatment for severe depression. It was not costly, most standard health insurance plans covered it, and hospitals profited from its use. The Harvard Medical School psychiatrist Alan Stone recalled that as late as the 1960s, 'the blue bloods in Boston would go to McLean's [private hospital] and receive psychotherapy. The working-class Irish Catholics would go to St. Elizabeth's Hospital and get shock therapy.'" [3]

3.25

In retrospect, it seems probable that my mother-in-law's illness, like my own mother's, was post-partum in nature, although it was never characterized as such; the youngest of her three children was only 9 months old when she was hospitalized. She lost, or relinquished, custody of the children (the legalities were not openly discussed in the family) and, after a period of supervised visits, she became a weekend parent. Although not permanently estranged, her three children have never forgiven her. What I am still unable to discern, after 20-plus years of intimate affiliation, is whether they can't forgive the mother that she wasn't—or the mother that she was.

3.26

What I'm trying to say is this: whether nature or nurture, or neither or both; whether genetic or epigenetic; whether intergenerational trauma or the cost of surviving in a world in which some nameless stranger who jerks off into a sterile cup for quick cash feels entitled to publicize his disgust at the possibility of your conception; my daughter's illness can feel, at times, overdetermined. What we used to call fate.

3.27

All the boys are here for anger issues, K told me during her second (or was it third?) hospitalization; *all the girls for self-harm*.

I imagine it will come as no shock to the reader that both my partner and I have, from time to time, also suffered from depression, although neither of us has ever been hospitalized for the illness. Like K, I tend more toward anxiety. Other people's depression seems to intensify my anxiety, as when my partner sleeps late, say, after 10:00 am, which she does most days unless a specific commitment compels her to wake early. Some mornings, I find myself disgusted by this behavior. Some mornings, I find myself disgusted, but I do not call her a disgusting pig.

3.29

I restrain myself.

3.30

I restrain myself, though the words do come to mind, and my lips do form their outline.

3.31

An amendment to a previous assertion: whereas it is true that, all those years ago, when we stopped having sex, it was because we were angry with one another, it is *also* true that we were disgusted by one another. I remember that my touch had become an issue. The rough texture of my fingers and hands had become intolerable to her, which I found strange. My touch had never been a problem in any prior relationship, and so I distrusted the complaint. Still, I moisturized daily, frequently. Resentfully, I kept a bottle of lotion next to the bed. But, no matter: always the same recoiling. Which seemed crazy to me, evidence of her lack of self-awareness, her refusal to take responsibility for her feelings. Thus, through this narrow vector—my stubbornness and hers—disgust entered our relationship. Entered and expressed itself.

3.32

Perhaps disgust has no real opposite. Perhaps its function is to reveal how the oppositions that structure our daily lives are not oppositions at all, but continuums upon which we must slip and slide, slip and slide, ceaselessly falling into the muck. Perhaps disgust knows that corruption is always at hand, that separateness is a pretense, a lie. And because disgust knows what we daily try to refuse—that we all must die—it expresses itself, when it expresses itself, with great confidence.

3.33

When I was twelve years old, I experienced my first panic attacks. I had begun to question my faith, which is to say, night after night I asked god to reveal himself to me, to reassure me of his existence, but he refused. The attacks were ice-cold, debilitating, solitary. Eventually, I learned to distract myself from the panic until it lessened or abated. In high school, I learned not to smoke weed, which precipitated its tachycardia with a vengeance. In college, I learned to embrace existentialism, whose intellectual severity perfectly echoed the puritanism of my upbringing, and whose logic recast my panic as a kind of sophistication. In other words, *la nausée* is not a new subject for me, not at all.

3.34

As part of my embrace of existentialism, I studied French. For a year, I lived in Paris, where I briefly took up smoking, and where no French person, male or female, expressed the slightest interest in me. I worked as an au pair and read Simone de Beauvoir novels. My favorite, *L'Invitée* was about a cosmopolitan couple who had an open relationship, which meant the man had other lovers and the woman didn't mind. A pretty American from my same study-abroad program made money by posing nude for an art class held in the artist's home. She encouraged me to do the same and gave me his number. I was large-bodied and awkward. During the interview, as we discussed the job of holding poses naked while others stared, the artist asked me to undress. I had acne on my chest and shoulders. Somehow my existentialism did not translate well into French; did not communicate what I hoped it would. He never called me back.

I am trying—has the reader already guessed?—to understand my own interest in disgust, as if it were a choice. As if it, too, weren't overdetermined. After French came Freud, but how is he not another sharp turn in the same direction? As a feminist, as a mother of daughters, I feel the need to clarify that the Freud I love is not the Freud of the seduction theory and penis envy, but the Freud of narrative and metaphor, of language and association. The Freud of lying on that slender couch week after week and telling and re-telling the story of one's life. The Freud of self-fashioning. If my mother were alive, she'd say you can't pick and choose, which was also what she said about Catholicism. But, of course, we all do, all the time, pick and choose. In order to live in this world, we must. Perhaps the opposite of disgust, if disgust has an opposite, is compassion.

Friends have asked what in particular provoked my mother's rage, incited her use of *disgusting pigs*. It's as difficult to say as it is to parse a single instance of her disgust, which, like her love, we experienced as pervasive. I think it probable that she said this when she felt overwhelmed by her role as a housewife; when she realized that none of us were helping her with the drudgery of maintaining our home, that is, with the intimate domestic labor that sustained our class position.

3.37

It's true that none of us helped her very much. We did this and that, the dishes after supper, an occasional session of vacuuming until the vacuum broke, after which I would get on my hands and knees to clean the wall-to-wall carpet, to collect the accumulated lint and hair and crumbs, although nothing could be done about the layer of grime that had settled into the nubby pile. I vacuumed-by-hand most mornings, before school, so that when she raged at us, when my mother's mouth turned down in furious contempt, I could allow myself to feel, for that day, at least, temporarily (temporarily) exempt.

3.38

These days, I find myself wondering how she was able to return to loving us after such intense bouts of revulsion. By what mechanism? Weeks passed before she did: return to us. Or so I thought. Recently, my sister told me it was only days. Days! But you know how time works for kids; you know how days can feel like years. Like a lifetime, really.

4 Origins

When I was six years old, I was hospitalized for pneumonia. Although my memory of the event is partial, it has stayed vivid. I remember the see-through oxygen tent under which I was confined for several days; I remember disobeying the nurses to leave its sanctity; I remember a bossy girl, lean and knowledgeable, a hospital veteran who was allowed to roam the halls, with whom I fell in love; I remember refusing the undignified bedpan and sneaking, light-headed, to the over-bright bathroom, mercifully *en suite*, in order to relieve myself properly; I remember the visit from young Father Daley, my favorite priest, who wore a Jesus beard and brought a wrapped Christmas present from underneath the parish tree where gifts were left for the poor; and I remember being separated from my mother.

4.2

My missing her took the form of a hideous lump in my throat, whose particular pain I can still recall. I was so small at the time, and my longing for her so acute, the lump constricted the passageway: it hurt to breathe or speak or swallow. Most of all, it hurt to cry, which I was incapable of forestalling, although the admonishment to contain my feelings—*you're a big girl now*—was sounded by every nurse, doctor, and family member I encountered. My inability to comply with this demand felt like a great moral failure, which led me to apologize continually. I apologize still.

4.3

So, the memory: I am sitting up in bed—the oxygen tent has recently been removed and the texture-less air is a kind of foothold where I cannot gain purchase—I am sitting up and snatching at the air and listening for the familiar clap of my mother's heel against hospital linoleum. Time has accordion-ed out, in the cruel way that it does, lengthening in precise relation to the intensity of my desire that it shrink. The wait is surely a punishment for my extravagant love for my mother: she who does not encourage extravagance of any kind.

4.4

At the first recognizable clap, the hideous lump overtakes my throat: I mustn't cry. I mustn't, but I do, and the humiliation is like a knife I must swallow around. All at once, I do not want her to come. I do not want her to come because her coming will only mean her leaving again, which I cannot bear. Her coming will compress her visit to nothingness and expand the hours apart so we will never see each other again. I realize with sudden clarity that the only way to survive this separation is to lengthen it; the only way to *not* never see her again is to *not* see her now! But my calculations and strategies, my hysterical insights and judicious feelings are swept aside, they do not matter, they never matter, and this is the real pain of childhood.

4.5

The clapping stills, and I glance up and there she is, my mother, filling the doorway. She is very Irish-looking, although I do not know that then, because I don't know what Irish is. Black Irish, which means skin more tawny than fair, deep brown eyes and dark hair, and teeth, once straightened, that lately have preferred to crowd. She smiles. How could I ever have not wanted her to come? She steps into the room and together, together at last, we weep.

5 Orders of Protection

The first mistake most parents make—bear with me here—is to misunderstand the purpose and function of the handcuffs. As counterintuitive as it seems, the handcuffs are provided for your child's protection, her safety; they are not meant as punishment for, or as expressions of disgust regarding, her mental illness. Bear with me here. Required by the county, the handcuffs are meant to protect her, to keep her from harming herself in the backseat of the sheriff's car, the one transporting her (also required) from the Emergency Room to which you rushed her to a psychiatric hospital that will treat her depression or trauma or anxiety, or some unfathomable combination of the three; the sheriff's car with the hard and slippery plastic seat on which she will find it nearly impossible to sit upright and maintain a familiar posture, one recognizable to herself or to her parents, now watching curbside, bewildered, as the black and tan vehicle pulls away. Technically, the handcuffs are to prevent her from running, from escaping the locked sheriff's car, whose front seat is occupied by two armed deputies, one of whom is female, both of whom fear your daughter's potential escape could cause her further self-injury, not to mention tremendous embarrassment to them personally, and to the department as a whole. Truth be told, it's the foot shackles, not the handcuffs, that prevent escape, the foot shackles that make running implausible and walking difficult, a slow, forward-leaning shuffle. If any part of this carceral experience produces shame (not by design, of course, but by happenstance), it is the foot shackles and the strange, halting gait they require. This gait is identifiable to those in the know, which includes the ER hospital staff, as well as some, but by no means all, poor families, migrant families, black and brown families, that is, families who are, for myriad reasons, already intimate with the criminal justice system. But it's puzzling to those fortunates who haven't before seen their 13- or 14- or 15-year-old child making slow progress down a hospital corridor, one flat-faced deputy on either side. Indeed, the foot shackles and the shuffling gait come as a terrible surprise to those parents—usually white, usually middle-class and above—who expect their absolute authority over the bodies and minds of their children to be universally respected; the parents who, like myself and, perhaps, like some of you, have never before been in an adversarial position toward the state and whose children have never before been objects of institutional disgust.

If and when these parents continue to plead their case—our voices at first tinny and wheedling, then gravel-edged, threatening—the deputies will become only more flat-faced, only more indifferent-seeming. But, let me assure you, indifferent they are not: they can't afford to be. Their jobs, let's be honest, their jobs are extraordinarily difficult, not well-paid, their purview includes transporting prisoners to and from the local jail, as well as chauffeuring the mentally ill to psychiatric facilities across the state. The deputies are providing a service, think of it that way; besides, the county requires it; besides, they themselves don't make, they only enforce, the rules. And the rules are firm, they are iron-clad, non-negotiable. If the sheriff's deputies appear cruelly inflexible, if they refuse to treat your exceptional child as an evident exception, it's not because they are heartless, but because they know too well that mental illness is a blight quite like poverty, which is to say, a blight with a quality of contagion that threatens to pull everyone within reach—patients and parents and deputy sheriffs alike—down, forever down, into the muck. In conclusion, then, as a parent who has survived this ordeal not once, not twice, not—bear with me here—I wish to reassure you, as well as myself, that in no way, shape, or form are the handcuffs and foot shackles intended to criminalize your daughter's mental illness. There is not now, and never has been, a hospital-to-prison pipeline; and there is no reason, none at all, rest assured, truth be told, to feel ashamed.

6 Guardian of the Mouth

6.1

These days, my body is always sore. K's body is always sore. In our house, we call this soreness *Old Man-itus*. We three are afflicted: K, her other mom, and me. At night, we creep, hunched and bow-legged, from room to room, forgetting what we came for. We came to give each other solace. To banish, if temporarily, the *Old Man-itus*. We climb in bed together and talk and tell stories until K falls asleep. The number of hospitalizations has climbed to eight.

The new crop of therapists—mostly behaviorists who disdain Freud—have explained to us that emotion is experienced not, as our language suggests, solely by the heart, or, as recent science suggests, by the brain, but throughout the entire body. *Really?* In other words, we have *Old Man-itus* because we are afraid. Our bodies have been depleted by the effort of keeping fear at bay. As a result, we can hardly risk feeling anything at all. I feign regular feelings quite well. I feign affect like a champ, like a professional. At work, lately, I excel. My colleagues admire my efficaciousness. I despise everyone whose child is well. I am good at hiding this feeling. It is my chief pleasure, my singular joy: both the despising and my expert hiding of it.

6.3

I have a writer friend who is dying. He has been dying for many years, but, as of late, lives in near-constant pain. Already, he has survived many traumas, some personal, some historical. When we get together, we talk about our spectacularly difficult mothers. Also: mental illness. Also: our diminishing sex lives. And, of course, disgust.

He reminds me that disgust contains attraction: what repels also compels. Although I don't doubt the wisdom of this observation—it pervades the disgust literature—I have trouble locating the feeling of desiring what disgusts me. (Apparently this is what is meant by *the unconscious*.) What I love about my friend is his absolute embrace of all his feelings, including the ugliest ones. His life-long proximity to death—his father died suddenly when he was 11; then his favorite brother, an overdose; then his own addiction and the endless AIDS crisis; then a liver transplant (to treat the same illness that took his father)—this proximity has made him uninterested in self-censure, in small-talk, in politesse. What a relief it is to be in his presence.

6.5

He has always claimed some self-disgust at being homosexual. This claim is, at once, performance, hyperbole, and truth.

6.6

The beliefs about homosexuality that that my writer friend and I grew up with coincide perfectly with the contagion view of disgust: namely that one was *turned into* a homosexual via homosexual sex, and that a single encounter was all it took. "The law of contagion operates according to the principle of 'once in contact, always in contact,' in that previously benign objects can acquire enduring, even permanent infectious qualities after even brief contact with a disgusting stimulus.... For instance, individuals will often refuse to drink from a glass that has been repeatedly and thoroughly sanitized if it had once been used to hold dog feces...." [1]

My mother's disgust at my sexuality was imbued
with this strange belief, which researchers call
sympathetic magic.[2] My first novel came out the
year she died, at age 68, of ovarian cancer. In the run
up to publication, we argued about the book jacket
and, later, the acknowledgments page, both of which
revealed that I was a lesbian. *You should be ashamed*,
she said, paging through the novel for the first time.
Two months before she died, she asked me to remove
the offending material. I told her I could not. *My
friends will desert me if they know*, she said. *Can't you
wait until after I'm dead?*

6.8

The novel to which my mother objected, *The Passion of Alice*, is about a woman who almost dies from anorexia. I've never suffered from this illness, but I was a compulsive overeater for many years. What the various eating disorders share, despite their differences in behaviors and outcomes—what the 98-pound woman shares with her 160-pound or 400-pound sister—is a deep sense of her own greediness. The shame of wanting, of rapacious need, of the bottomless, bottomless pit. The shame, if you will, of having a body at all.

6.9

That shame is a product of disgust almost goes without saying, yet it still requires our attention. Shame is a product of disgust in the way that death is a product of life (inevitable), babies are a product of coitus (mysterious), and the food we eat—steak, say—is a product of slaughter (transformational).

6.10

Another writer friend—this one not actively dying, but a seeker, like myself, preparing for death through his work, as I am, have been, all my life, without quite realizing—he reminded me of the connections between disgust, shame, and religious practice: *death fear, food guilt, sex magic*, he wrote.

6.11

For many years, I searched for a place to lay blame for my eating disorder, a search that circled perpetually around my mother. I wanted the clarity of cause and effect. And, of course, I wanted relief. (Naively, I imagined the one would produce the other.) After years of struggle, I have come to view my own eating disorder as existential in nature, like my daughter's cutting, and my mother's debilitating postpartum depression: How do I live in this body? That is, how do I live in this *now*, in this body?

6.12

By making this assertion, I do not mean to flatten into sameness these three afflictions. Nor do I wish to elide the likelihood of specific trauma. Instead, I wish to view the female body as the stage on which these dramas—existential and traumatic; existential, perhaps, because traumatic—are played out.

6.13

In the last decade or so, the therapeutic community has embraced the term *disordered eating* because it affords the sufferer agency, acknowledges her responsibility for her behaviors, and respects the furious protest in what she does.

6.14

Take the baby and go find another wife.

6.15

All the boys are here for anger issues, all the girls for self-harm.

6.16

And what about the kids who identified as neither? According to K, the nonbinary kids and the trans boys and trans girls were usually housed in the girls' unit where, it was predicted, they'd be safer. Whatever emotional distress this decision caused the trans boys, it also protected them from those whose disgust response—whose insistence upon categorical purity—took the form of physical violence. K said that most of the trans kids didn't really mind because they already knew cis male violence. Their refusal to collude in the gender regime under which we all live, and variously suffer, had already provoked it.

6.17

The thing about collusion is, once you understand the mechanism—each holding an opposite pole—you begin to see it everywhere.

6.18

One of the theses of *The Passion of Alice*, is that eating disorders are part protest, part capitulation, to the demands our culture places on female bodies. If I were writing *Alice* today, I would frame it differently: all forms of protest come at great personal cost, but none more so than protests against the systems that structure how we see (and refuse to see) and experience (and refuse to experience) our own bodies and one another's.

6.19

At the height of my own disordered eating, when I overate, shame descended like a fugue: my vision narrowed, the lights dimmed, an unbearable weight seemed to press against my lungs and throat. I became a 2-D version of myself: flat, immobile, blank, execrable. This did not feel like protest; it felt like annihilation.

6.20

The word disgust comes from the Latin *dis*, opposite of, and *gustus*, taste, literally dis-taste. "[M]ost definitions of disgust appear to be related to the actual or threatened oral incorporation of contaminated or unwanted stimuli. Accordingly, it has been suggested that disgust may function primarily as a guardian of the mouth, thereby highlighting its uniqueness from other emotions." [3]

Guardian of the mouth! What a precise, near lyrical, way to describe anorexia. Here, disgust functions to prevent oral incorporation—not of things foreign or frightening or diseased—but of things nourishing and essential to life. It prevents the anorectic from becoming that which disgusts her: herself.

6.22

Guardian of the mouth also returns me to The Spy—as of course it must—who defended his own mouth with great vigilance. His disgust kept him alive, kept him from ingesting femaleness or death, which appeared to him to be one and the same.

6.23

But wouldn't a *guardian of the mouth* also be a protector of oral pleasures? A means, perhaps perversely, of claiming desire? A guardian of speech and language and prayer? Guardian of kissing and being kissed, of crying out, as I have, and perhaps the reader has, in ecstasy and in despair. Guardian of dick-sucking and pussy-eating; guardian of the mouth that sings; the mouth that praises and condemns; guardian of the mouth that rages, rages—the mouth of poetry. The holy, holy mouth.

6.24

Likely the astute reader has already surmised that I'm trying—however ham-handedly—to incorporate disgust, as my dying friend has. I'm trying to incorporate that feeling which defends against incorporation. And to abandon any effort to keep it at bay. If only to prevent another bout of *Old Man-itus*, I'm trying to embrace all my feelings, even, especially, the ugliest ones, as the Freudian therapist—have I told you her name was Pamela?—entreated me to, many years ago. *Pamela* is an invented name meaning *all sweetness*, which does not capture my Pamela—not at all. Loving someone requires much more than sweetness, requires a kind of grueling muscularity, and psychoanalysis, when practiced well, is one of our best means of enacting this. Together, Pamela and I invented the rest of my life.

6.25

By incorporating disgust, I'm trying to accept my own (nauseating) mortality, against which I have protested since adolescence, when those first, terrifying, ice-cold intimations of nothingness began to prick my consciousness. One panic attack from that time stands out in particular detail. It arrived during gym class, as we lined up to go outside. I can still see the enormous metal door that led to the asphalt path that led to the worn-out track, inside of which stood sickly yellow grass; I can still feel my jiggling girl's body jiggle, and how I hid my panic in the out-of-breath-ness of the run. Was it the intimation of nothingness, or my own mediocrity, that terrified?

6.26

"Caius is a man, men are mortal, therefore Caius is mortal—had seemed to [Ivan Ilyich] all his life correct only as regards Caius, but not at all as regards himself." [4]

In *The Passion of Alice*, the narrator is a recent convert to Catholicism who understands her anorexia as a kind of mortification of the flesh. Emulating Christ on the Cross, she attempts to starve away the shame of desiring. Might I point to the savage irony of my mother telling me I should be ashamed of a book I wrote about a woman dying of shame?

6.28

Both of my writer friends, the one dying and the one preparing to, were raised Catholic, like myself; this is part of why, or perhaps how, I love them. What is Catholicism if not an education in the power of metaphor? Resurrection, transubstantiation, original sin: *death fear, food guilt, sex magic.*

6.29

I am struck by the extent to which metaphor, rather than simile, captures the experience of shame[5]: it equates, rather than compares, one thing to another. I am not *like* the disgusting thing; I am the thing itself. As well the experience of psychosis: it is not *as if* the television were talking to me, I'm already answering back. In each instance, a contagion of meaning.

Or, to take it a step further, Catholicism is to metaphor, as Protestantism is to simile: this *is* the body of Christ. My writer friends' Catholic childhoods were, like mine, variously precarious, meaning variously loving and variously not. And yet there it was, all along, in our midst: the body and blood, the blood and the body, the key to the locked door leading out. *This is how language works! This is a how to become something, someone, you are not!*

6.31

Were she still alive, perhaps my mother would point to the savage irony of my figuring Catholicism as, in any way, metaphorical.

6.32

In 1968, when I was six years old, Pope Paul VI issued *Humanae Vitae*, an encyclical which declared that "[The church] considers it lawful for married people to take advantage of the infertile period [of a woman's cycle] but condemns as always unlawful the use of means which directly prevent conception, even when the reasons given for the later practice may appear to be upright and serious."[6]

6.33

Had my mother used birth control, her reasons would have been both upright and serious. Five years passed between her first child and her second. She must have been afraid—both she and my father must have been terrified—of another debilitating postpartum depression. What courage it must have taken to have sex at all when she knew where it might lead her.

6.34

"Consciousness is lost immediately after the shock button is pressed and the fit occurs instantly at an interval up to one minute in duration... The tonic generalized contraction is associated with flushing of the face... followed by the clonic phase which may be associated with involuntary defecation and... frothing at the mouth." [7]

6.35

Would it be romantic of me to say that I write in order to transubstantiate my mother's shame? By *romantic* I mean *untrue*.

6.36

By *untrue* I mean: a story I tell myself to feel better.

6.37

If, according to Mary Douglas, "ritual makes visible external signs of internal states"[8] and if, according to Catholic doctrine, the ritual of transubstantiation affirms, without explaining, the fact of Christ's presence; might it be true that I'm trying to affirm, via language, my mother's impossible presence in a way that does not annihilate me?

6.38

By *annihilate me*, I mean: *Can't you wait until after I'm dead?*

Three months after *The Passion of Alice* was published, my mother died at home, surrounded by her husband and two daughters. For days, she threw up black bile from her hospital bed in the living room. I've an almost cartoon memory of my sister racing back and forth to the toilet to empty the putrid bucket. She and I had failed to deliver our mother's Compazine, an anti-nausea med, frequently enough to suppress her vomiting. Ultimately, we had to provide the Compazine via suppositories because she could not swallow the medicine. Glycerin suppositories and lime green popsicles and liquid morphine placed, via a medical eye dropper, onto her tongue: these were how we loved her. These were the material proofs of the grueling muscularity of our love.

6.40

Perhaps it goes without saying that my mother's friends did not desert her once they learned I was a lesbian. Nor did she manage to relinquish her disgust before she died. It turns out that disgust and love are not incompatible, not at all. Instead, each feeling creates space for the other: there is no intimacy without disgust. And this is the real pain of our relationships.

6.41

What to incorporate, then, what to push away? What of disgust to—if not quite embrace—then recognize as clear indications of who we are and where our values lie? And what to reject as dishonesty and self-deception, as the inability to accept the finite reality of our terribly human lives?

6.42

K has not been suicidal for more than two years. We no longer suffer from *Old Man-itus*, although this does not mean that everyone in the house sleeps well. Loosed from K, the self-disgust that once plagued her has managed somehow to migrate, to seek out and inhabit one or the other of us, although never quite in the same devastating way. Still, we are all susceptible, each family member; perhaps because we are fatigued, perhaps because we are female, perhaps because we are, each of the four, daughters of flawed mothers; and perhaps because, against all reason, we have persisted in these bodies, whose contagion of meaning appears to be without end.

Endnotes

Epigraph

1   Douglas, Mary. *Purity and Danger: An Analysis of the Concepts of Pollution and Taboo*. Routledge, 1984, p. 165.

The Man Who Would Not Kiss

1   Tyber, J. M., D. Lieberman, and V. Griskevicius. "Microbes, mating, and morality: Individual differences in three functional domains of disgust." *Journal of Personality and Social Psychology*, vol. 97, no. 1, 2009, pp. 103–22.

2   I owe much of my thinking here, and elsewhere in this book, to William Miller's *The Anatomy of Disgust*, an extraordinary meditation that draws from psychology, history, literature, and philosophy.

3   Miller, William. *The Anatomy of Disgust*. Harvard University Press, 1997, p. 2.

4   Douglas, Mary, p. 2.

5   Miller, William. p. 15.

6   Ibid, p. 32.

7   Freud, Sigmund. "The Most Prevalent Forms of Degradation in Erotic Life," in *Collected Papers*, edited by Jean Riviere and James Strachey. *The International Psycho-Analytical Library* 4, p 213.

8   Freud, Sigmund. *Three Essays on the Theory of Sexuality*, in *The Standard Edition of the Complete Psychological Works of Sigmund Freud*, edited by James Strachey. Hogarth Press, 1953-1974, p. 152.

Self-Disgust

1   Rozin, Paul, L. Lowery, and R. Ebert. "Varieties of disgust faces and the structure of disgust." *Journal of Personality and Social Psychology*, vol. 66, no. 5, 1994, pp. 870-881. More recent research challenges the idea that emotions reliably correspond to specific facial expressions. *See* Barrett, Lisa Feldman. *How Emotions Are Made*. Houghton Mifflin Harcourt, 2017, pp. 4-12.

2   Rozin, Paul, and April Fallon. "A Perspective on Disgust," *Psychological Review*, vol 94. no. 1, 1987, p. 38.

3   Harrington, Anne. *Mind Fixers: Psychiatry's Troubled Search for the Biology of Mental Illness*. W.W. Norton, 2019, p. 187.

Guardian of the Mouth

1   Olatuniji, B. O., and C. N. Sawchuk. "Disgust: Characteristic Features, Social Manifestations,

and Clinical Implications." *Journal of Social and Clinical Psychology*, vol. 24, no. 7, 2005, pp. 932-962.

2   Rozin, Paul, L. Millman, and C. Nemeroff. "Operation of the Laws of Sympathetic magic in Disgust and Other Domains." *Journal of Personality and Social Psychology*, vol. 50, no. 4, 1986, pp. 703-712.

3   Ibid.

4   Tolstoy, Leo. *The Death of Ivan Ilyich*. Boni & Liveright, 2004, p. 41.

5   Gratitude to literary scholar David Pike who offered this insight as well as the SAT analogy on the following page.

6   Paul VI. "Humanae Vitae: Encyclical Letter of Pope Paul VI on the Regulation of Birth." New Advent, July 25, 1968, https://www.newadvent.org/library/docs_pao6hv.htm

7   Ryan, V. Gerard, and Lucie Jessner. *Shock Treatment in Psychiatry: A Manual*, Grune & Stratton, 1941.

8   Douglas, Mary, p. 70.

Works Consulted

Barrett, Lisa Feldman. *How Emotions Are Made: The Secret Life of the Brain*. Houghton Mifflin Harcourt, 2017.

Douglas, Mary. *Purity and Danger: An Analysis of the Concepts of Pollution and Taboo*. Routledge, 1984.

Ekman, Paul, and H. Oster. "Facial Expressions of Emotion." *Annual Review of Psychology*, vol. 30, 1979, pp. 527-554.

Freud, Sigmund. *Three Essays on the Theory of Sexuality*, in *The Standard Edition of the Complete Psychological Works of Sigmund Freud*, edited by James Strachey. Hogarth Press, 1953-1974.

———. *Collected Papers*, edited by Joan Riviere and James Strachey. *The International Psycho-Analytical Library* 4, 1924-50.

Harrington, Anne. *Mind Fixers: Psychiatry's Troubled Search for the Biology of Mental Illness*. W.W. Norton, 2019.

Miller, William. *The Anatomy of Disgust*. Harvard University Press, 1997.

Ngai, Sianne. *Ugly Feelings*. Harvard University Press, 2005.

Nussbaum, Martha. *Hiding from Humanity: Disgust, Shame and the Law*. Princeton University Press, 2004.

Olatuniji, B.O., and C.N. Sawchuk. "Disgust: Characteristic Features, Social Manifestations, and Clinical Implications." *Journal of Social and Clinical Psychology*, vol. 24, no. 7, 2005, pp. 932-962.

Phillips, Adam. *Becoming Freud: The Making of a Psychoanalyst*. Yale University Press, 2014.

Paul VI. "Humanae Vitae: Encyclical Letter of Pope Paul VI on the Regulation of Birth." New Advent, July 25, 1968, https://www.newadvent.org/library/docs_pao6hv.htm

Rozin, Paul, and April Fallon. "A Perspective on Disgust," *Psychological Review,* vol 94. no. 1, 1987, pp. 23-41.

Rozin, Paul, J. Haidt, and C. McCauley. "Disgust" in *Handbook of Emotions*, edited by Michael Lewis and Jeannette M. Haviland. Guilford Press, 1993.

Rozin, Paul, L. Lowery, and R. Ebert. "Varieties of disgust faces and the structure of disgust." *Journal of Personality and Social Psychology*, vol. 66, no. 5, 1994, pp. 870-881.

Rozin, Paul, L. Millman, and C. Nemeroff. "Operation of the Laws of Sympathetic magic in Disgust and Other Domains." *Journal of Personality and Social Psychology*, vol. 50, no. 4, 1986, pp. 703-712.

Ryan, V. Gerard, and Lucie Jessner. *Shock Treatment in Psychiatry: A Manual*, Grune & Stratton, 1941.

Tolstoy, Leo. *The Death of Ivan Ilyich*. Boni & Liveright, 2004.

Tyber, J. M., D. Lieberman, and V. Griskevicius. "Microbes, mating, and morality: Individual differences in three functional domains of disgust." *Journal of Personality and Social Psychology*, vol. 97, no. 1, 2009, pp. 103–22.

Acknowledgments

This small book has benefited from a phalanx of insightful and generous readers who labored over parts, or all, of the manuscript, including many colleagues at American University: David Keplinger, Keith Leonard, Dolen Perkins-Valdez, David Pike, Melissa Scholes-Young, Aram Sinnreich, Richard Sha, and Rachel Louise Snyder; and many writers from my life before and beyond AU: Karin Cook, Jaime Grant, Michael Leavett, Richard McCann, Molly McGinnis, Catherine McKinley, Honor Moore, Hanna Pylväinen, Elizabeth Roberts, and Jacqueline Woodson. I'm especially indebted to David Keplinger, who was the first to suggest these writings might be a book; and to anthropologist and prince consort Ara Wilson, whose capacity to think structurally about issues great and small, sacred and profane, is an ongoing revelation. I could not have had a smarter, kinder, or more fun team than the good people at Scuppernong Editions in Greensboro, North Carolina: Steve Mitchell, Brian Lampkin, Andrew Saulters, and the delightful Deonna Kelli Sayed. I am immensely grateful to these readers and friends for their embrace of disgust and for the late Richard McCann's admonishment to think harder and to feel more. Always more.

Stephanie Grant is the author of the novels, *The Passion of Alice* and *Map of Ireland*. She currently directs the MFA Program in Creative Writing at American University.

Advance Praise for *Disgust: A Memoir*

"In this condensed, profound contemplation of disgust, Stephanie Grant traces the complexity and fearfulness of intergenerational conflict and touches on the transmissibility (or not) of mental illness. Her meditations read like prose poems, each economically summoning another intricacy of her subject. She moves with unusual grace between the universal and the highly specific, revealing startling truths about love and fear and anger and pain and redemption."

ANDREW SOLOMON, author of *Far and Away* and *The Noonday Demon*

"Part psychoanalytical commentary on the forms and manifestations of the disgust impulse, part personal essay, what is brilliant about the work is exactly what makes it so unsettling, as Grant traverses arenas that range from social scientists' engagement with the three domains of disgust—pathogenic, sexual, and moral—to 'a man who will not kiss,' to her own mother's disgust response to homosexuality."

DAVID KEPLINGER, *The World to Come*

First printing
ISBN 978-1-7329328-5-2

DESIGN. Text in Fournier. Titles in Avenir. Cover
design, cover photography, and interior design by
Andrew Saulters. Scuppernong Editions colophon by
Rachel York.

Sections of Chapter 3 and Chapter 6 have appeared
in *The New Yorker Online* in a slightly different form.

Scuppernong Editions offers the occasional
publication of adventuresome, commercially
questionable writing in all genres.

Scuppernong Editions
304 South Elm Street
Greensboro, NC 27401

CPSIA information can be obtained
at www.ICGtesting.com
Printed in the USA
LVHW080028040222
710079LV00011B/421